MOTHERS TABOO

MOTHERS TABOO

Horrendously honest poems on motherhood.

Honestly.

By Leander Moore

CONTENTS

MOTHERS TABOO

All those things I wanted to say

All those things we go through every day.

All those thoughts I've wanted to get off of my chest.

The things that happen to those who try their best.

The realities, The testimonies,

The bloody sh t storm in a cup.

We've all been there thinking that we've truly f cked it up.

Birth, stitches, unwelcome advice,

Friends, family (the 'oldies' to be precise)

Sex, relationships and overfilled boobs.

Well, here's my truth about motherhood.

Full of things aloud we cannot say,

In front of the kids at a stay and play.

If you're offended easily, these poems aren't for you.

But I hope you enjoy reading, 'Mothers Taboo'.

MUMMY?

In the last minute

He has said mummy over

Twenty-seven times.

I'M SORRY

Bath bombs. Tampons.

Thrush. Sex.

Tampons. Thursh.

Smear tests. Sex.

Pregnancy.

In anger you puffed out the veins

Surrounding your entrance

Like tiny walls of defense.

It made sense.

Then, childbirth.

And to top it all off, after all that you've done,

I signed up to a spin class.

Now both my vagina and my arse

hate me.

GIVE IT A TRY

Stop with the crap

That leaves your mouth.

"Here, let me do it my way."

I just want the chance

To give it a shot;

I'll have to succeed someday.

Say, "Give it a try

and if you get stuck

then feel free to give me a shout."

Don't just try taking over,

You've no 'Magic Touch'

Otherwise I'll end up kicking you out.

"YOU LOOK TIRED"

What a perfectly sh t

Comment to make

When they know you've been up most the night.

Don't just shrug it off,

Make a comment back;

You're perfectly within your right.

My personal favourite

Is "No sh t, Sherlock."

Or, "Thanks. You've ruined my day."

Or tell them, "You look fat" -

See how they take that.

"You look tired" is a sh t thing to say.

SECOND HAND SUE

Get it scuffed

Get it scraped

See how many holes you can make.

Tear the knees

Tear the sleeves

See which buttons you can break.

Questionable stains

Paint on veins,

There's a reason we don't buy brand new.

Searching charity shops,

Hand-me-down drops,

Less stress thanks to Second-hand Sue.

EAT THE CAKE

Four weeks postpartum

Dieting started

Still breastfeeding

Running around bleeding

Trying to get things together

Not finding any pleasure

In healthy foods.

My fluctuating moods

Kicked in.

I found the biscuit tin.

And the chocolate.

And the cake.

For goodness sake.

Eat the damn cake.

You've the rest of your life to be thin.

Right now, you're parenting.

Eat the damn cake.

POSTPARTUM SEX

Have you don't it yet?

They ask you six weeks after.

I'm not surprised if every woman

Answered in just laughter.

JUST LIKE THE FIRST TIME, BUT NOT

A bottle of champagne

To drown the fear of pain.

The lights down low,

But enough light to show

A sleeping face in the distance.

That was my insistence.

Our darkest sheets

In case blood should leak.

An expectation

Brief anticipation.

A nervousness heavy in the air

But no trace of sexy underwear.

More mechanical than before,

A re-connection. Something more.

No worlds were rocked.

But a door unlocked.

ACTIONS ARE LOUDER

Mid-morning wake ups at two weeks old

Desperate for those warm arms to fold

Around her body and hold her tight

For no other reason except she's alone at night.

Actions are her price.

Words do not suffice.

A tumble, a graze, a flood of tears

Not the first time and, at 4 years

Old, he knows what will make it better

And it's not a string of connected letters.

A swooping action

Taking just a fraction

Of time.

Standing in front of the school gates,

Unsure what uncertainty awaits,

A mother squeezes the small hand with her own,

Overwhelmed by how quickly they've grown.

She squeezes her hand back.

Sometimes words just lack

The intensity.

He's heard his wife's long speech,

Her actions disjointed from what she'd preached

Leaving them both feeling lonelier than ever before;

Wanting actions, not words, nothing more.

But followed by

The soft click of the door.

And yet when we were four

Actions were automatic.

NOTHING TO GIVE

Running on empty.

Nothing left.

Hollow.

SUNSHINE WINE

Afternoon drinking

Isn't much fun

With a boy who's three

And a girl who's one.

You can't get on it

Like we did years ago,

Because of these small people

We now have in tow.

Just let me confirm

We don't let them drink.

We're not bad mothers,

Not that we care what you think.

But if we've had a rough week,

Or it's sunny outside,

Or we want to slag off

The men on *Don't Tell the Bride*

We expect to be able to crack open a bottle,

Capable of parenting at full throttle:

Capable of supervising the kids.

And have a few drinks.

YOU THINK YOU GOT IT RIGHT

What's the weather like up there

On your throne or golden chair?

Or are you on your highest horse

Looking down on us of course?

You preach you know the only way

To raise a child, but may I say

That the job you did wasn't great,

In fact, if I should tell it straight,

I don't know how he's still alive

Because, probably until he was 35

You've washed his sheets, and combed his hair,

You've bought him socks and new underwear.

You've made each lunch and dinner too

In fact, if I'm honest, because of you

I feel like I'm a mum of two.

So, get down from your mighty height,

Your own parenting skills are quite a fright.

TAMPONS

That thing isn't going up there.

VPL? I really don't care.

My vag has been through enough;

She's experienced a lot and it's been kinda of rough.

Stretch and sweep, cervical screen,

A forceps birth and all in-between.

The last thing that passed through my cervix, cried...

Sorry, no tampons allowed inside.

HOME-SCHOOL

Today we focused on opposites.

I asked the kids to get ready,

They didn't.

Success!

PJ TIME

Today has been tough.

I've just had enough.

I'm in my pjs already,

With the wine pouring steady

The kids have been twats

I'm going to bed.

ACCIDENTAL LEAKAGE

I try and hold it

But don't think that I can

A lack of bladder control

Was not part of the plan.

A sneeze, a jump

Might end with a dribble

A cough, a scare

And I'm standing in piddle.

SLEEP?

I swear my kids have a rota

To deprive me of my sleep quota

She'll wake up to feed.

He'll wake 'cause he's peed.

I'm going to sleep on the sofa.

CLITOSAURUS

In the beginning, the Clitosaurus was King.

A happily dominant, plaything.

It thrived on touch and stimulation,

Regularly enjoying time and affection.

But that tickle, that touch was soon redeployed

Whilst bulging veins erupted; angered, annoyed.

Clitosaurus' fate followed a similar tale

Because after the arrival of the flesh that wailed,

She was demoted from King, excused from play,

Understandably ignored; she'd hear *her* say:

"I've got a headache." Or "I'm too tired tonight."

"I'm still not ready, I'm sorry, alright."

Exhausted of touch or stimulation,

Robbed of time and fatigued affection.

JUST A LITTLE PART

A little part of me wants you to:

... grow up and move out.

... be calm at nappy change, not kick about.

... never grow old.

... just do as you're told.

... freeze so I can take a cute photo.

... hold onto my hand and never let go.

... not bounce on my bladder every morning at 4.

... throw up over the mother in law.

... sleep. Every night. For at least 12 hours.

... be blessed with 'good baby' powers.

... express your opinion and enjoy being you.

... but always do what your mother tell you to.

IF THEY'RE CRYING THEY'RE STILL ALIVE

Dragging the bouncer to the bathroom door,

Using the tracks in the carpet from before,

He gurgled, supervising my brief encounter

With the shampoo, soap and shower.

You see, I was absolutely petrified

That out of my sight, he would have died.

But the best advice, from a mum-of-five,

"If they're crying then they're still alive!"

LITTLE ASSHOLES

Beautiful little assholes.

Drawing on the wall.

Beautiful little assholes.

Ripping paper in the hall.

Beautiful little assholes.

Making such a bloody mess.

Beautiful little assholes.

Wiping snot on to my dress.

Beautiful little assholes.

Not doing as they're told.

Beautiful little assholes.

Won't eat it cause it's cold.

Beautiful little assholes.

Won't f cking go to bed.

Beautiful little assholes

Copy everything you've said.

Beautiful little assholes.

Your smiles make my heart feel funny.

Beautiful little assholes.

I'm so glad to be your mummy.

THE RACE

The stiff mum and the calm mum had a race.

All that stiff could do was shout disgrace.

She made comments to those she sees

Judging all with shameful ease,

But kind, calm mum, was not brought up that way.

She's looking out for other mums,

A smile in the night.

'Cause parenting is hard, it can be down right shite.

Oh no! Her friends are gone! Stiff mum can't carry on!

But kind, calm mum, she's happy in her ways.

WHERE'S MINE

Do I remember what you got the baby

When I'd spent 13 hours in labour

And hadn't slept for over 24 hours

And had to pretend like I actually wanted visitors?

No.

Do I remember what you got me?

Yes.

Nothing.

You got me nothing.

DIFFERENT

Don't think that I am a horrible person

Because our opinions aren't the same

Or I do things a different way to you

Or because I have a different aim.

Or that I have different family values

Or that I openly speak my mind

Or I measure success based on happiness.

Or I keep old treasures that I find.

Or that I raise my children differently.

Or I have different dreams to you.

Or I stick up for what is right,

Or I see things from a different view.

No, I'm not a horrible person,

Unless you truly p ss me off.

Then you'll see an entirely different side

.....

MORNING SICKNESS

But not in the first trimester

Like everyone else.

And not as soon as you woke up

Like everyone else.

And not solved by eating ginger

Like everyone else.

And not debilitating

Like everyone else.

But at lunchtime or later afternoon

When your stomach is slightly empty

And you wretch until nothing comes up.

Not triggered by anything

Apart from maybe a leaf flittering across the ground

Or a rain drop that is too loud

Of it being a Wednesday

Oh, and all in the third trimester

When your bump hinders your ability to reach over the toilet.

Like everyone else.

POSTPARTUM BODY

"You've still got a tummy."

Well, isn't that funny.

I gave birth only three days ago.

But you've got a tummy,

And you're not a Mummy...

So, what you're excuse you judgemental sh t?

A BOY WITHOUT A WILLY

The exact same feelings,

The exact same cravings,

Third trimester vomiting,

All at the front growing,

Completely imitating

My first pregnancy,

Left me dreaming, believing,

Secretly knowing.

Imagining

Standing by the back door, shouting

"Boys! It's dinner time".

But you arrived screaming,

Not what I was expecting,

Finding it disappointing

That your willy was missing.

Everything I'd been planning

Needed rearranging.

For this baby girl I was left holding.

THE THOUGHTS THAT WENT THROUGH MY HEAD

What if I split my stitches?

What if I need more stitches?

I've forgotten how to push.

I really don't want to push.

It might have shrunk in the last few minutes.

I've been in here for 45 minutes.

This is worse than childbirth.

Just relax. It's not childbirth.

It's going to be bigger than the baby.

They'll think I've abandoned my baby.

If I push too hard will my uterus fall out?

Will this thing ever come out?

I'm never eating again.

Will I ever be able to poo normally again?

ASBO TAG

He's got a little asbo tag

To ensure no-one can steal him.

So, do not take him off the ward

Or you'll be the one screaming.

ISN'T SHE BEAUTIFUL?

Family are always desperate

"Who do you think she resembles?"

I know I can have some fun with this

And confirm when they're all assembled:

I say,

"She looks like Winston Churchill,

With that angry screwed up face.

She has Danny Devito's neck,

(just a tyre of chub in place).

She's got John Legend's cheeks,

Under Karl Sinckler's nose

Expressions of Karl Pilkington,

And Frodo Baggins' toes."

But, ignoring me, they carry on

Pulling out the physical connections.

"She's got your chin." They declare

"Isn't she the image of perfection."

FLAWLESSLY PERFECT

Three scars on my vagina,

One longer than the other.

Twelve stripes from my thighs to my belly.

A thousand grey hairs,

in undesirable places,

And a tummy that wobbles like jelly.

Two sagging, deflated,

redundant breasts.

And a waist line that's structurally unsound.

A bladder that leaks

When I suggest I might sneeze,

And a face that is getting quite round.

It's a flawless image

I'm not trying to perfect.

But the honest body of 'I am a Mum'.

Not 'perfectly flawless'

But I'm still proud to say

That this body is second to **none**.

YOU'RE DOING ALRIGHT

There's nobody closer

To getting it right

Than a messy haired mum

Who's been up most the night.

VISITING TIMES

Stringent, for a reason.

Not flexible to suit you.

There to protect the mums,

Babies and staff.

No babies will be taken

Out of the ward

Just to meet you on your terms

Do not suggest it.

Do not expect it.

The rules apply to you.

BOGIES ON THE WALL

Do the homeware stores

Sell bogie-bits paint?

Or are my kids unable

To show a little constraint?

For my walls have a contour

Of miniature mountains

With a waterfall-effect

Creating snot-like fountains.

What happened to flicking them

Or eating them raw?

I'm not overly bothered

If they appear on the floor.

But on the walls at head-height,

They don't look the greatest.

Unless I frame, label and light them -

A masterpiece is created!

BE LIKE DAD

When my first child arrived,

And after a gruelling five-hour drive,

Dad busied himself in the kitchen.

Visitors came for the first meeting

Of the baby, a few days old,

Everyone wanting a hold.

Dad made everyone tea,

Whilst Mum helped me,

And as far as I could see,

The other visitors sat stone clad.

If only they were more like Dad.

HOTEL

Tempting.

One night.

In a hotel.

No one else there.

Just me, alone in bed.

With one thing on my mind.

Not governed by the bloody Gro-clock.

Waking up when I want to wake up.

SMOOCHING

You don't need to kiss him, all over his head,

Every second or every minute of the day.

In fact, I don't want you to spread all of your germs,

Plus, he hasn't been washed, anyway!

He's still covered in gunk from my vaginal fluid

And I'm sure you don't want that on your lips.

But more importantly, I am breastfeeding

and your disgusting germs will probably confuse my tits.

Otherwise my boobs will make antibodies

For your little sniffle instead of creating for him.

I can drop some in your tea, if you really fancy,

But if not, then stop the smooching.

MAKE YOUR OWN

A brew? Make your own f cking brew.

You have functioning hands don't you?

I've got a person attached to my boob

I'm really not in the entertaining mood.

I've just given birth, and my vagina is sore

 You'll find tea bags behind a cupboard door.

I've spent long enough making a baby;

I think for one day you can be the tea lady.

MY VILLAGE

Option One was premade

No welcome parade.

But fully formed and functional

Geographically practical.

All the right noises

Promising promises.

Offers to confide

Advice to guide.

Invites to lunches,

Ignoring hunches.

Trying to fit in.

Trying to be like them.

But no actual support for me.

Just cuddles with the baby.

Option Two was harder,

Having to travel a bit further

Out of my comfort zone,

A long way from home.

Puzzle pieces of new mums

Forming together, creating chums.

No promises made,

Made welcome to invade

Whenever. Wherever.

No judgement whatsoever.

Supporting each other,

Celebrating wins as a mother.

Celebrating our fails,

Exchanging gory details

With a prosecco or two.

Yes, this village will do.

To village #2: thank you.

For everything we've been through.

I love you.

LIFTED

My heart always melts

When you raise those chubby arms

To get into mine.

MUMMY!

Mummy?

Where are you, Mummy?

Mummy, are you asleep?

Mummy, I've done a poo.

Mummy?

Mummy, I don't want milk on my cereal.

Mummy, I don't have any milk on my cereal!

What does this dinosaur eat, Mummy?

Mummy, look at this.

Please, I have an ice cream, Mummy?

Mummy, ice cream is a breakfast food.

Mummy, I have two arms, Mummy.

Mummy, look at me.

Mummy?

Mummy, the baby is crying.

Mummy, where is Daddy, Mummy?

Mummy, the moon is big.

I'm cutting my carrots, Mummy.

Mummy, look at what I'm doing.

Look, Mummy.

Mummy?

Mummy?

Mummy, why do worms have no legs?

Mummy, are you busy?

You know what, Mummy?

Mummy, I've finished.

Look, Mummy.

Mummy, look.

Mummy?

Mummy, can I sit on your lap?

Mummy, can I talk to them?

Who is on the phone, Mummy?

Can I talk, Mummy?

Mummy, I'm hungry, Mummy.

Mummy, can I watch Nemo?

Mummy?

Psst, Mummy.

Look at the Nemo fish, Mummy.

Don't turn it off, Mummy.

Mummy, I want to watch it again!

Mummy, I'm sorry.

I didn't, Mummy.

Eat your dinner, Mummy.

Night, Mummy.

Mummy?

I love you, Mummy.

RETURN POLICY

On the odd occasion,

Normally when it is raining

And nobody is listening to anybody,

I contemplate

asking about the return policy.

Is it 14 days for a full refund?

28 days for an exchange?

Only a credit note if you leave it any longer?

"If you are not completely satisfied with your item..."

Did I get a receipt?

Well, kind of.

Do my green notes count?

MAT LEAVE HOLIDAY

Yes, it's exactly like a holiday

All day just feeling free,

Lounging around, relaxing

and drunk by half past three.

No stresses, care or worries

to bother me at night.

No routine to follow in the day,

Nor pressure to get it right.

I mean, it's mat leave, right?

"A year off work!", they say

Coffee, cake and social calls

And play dates every day.

"Enjoy this time." is on repeat,

 "Make the most of your time off."

They're deluded; for we all know

The first year's always rough.

Just imagine a travel agent's face,

When you book your mat leave rest;

A peacefully quiet, adult-only place

Because you do deserve the best.

Mat leave? A holiday? Pah!

A concept far from reality.

Maternity leave is a blur of sh t

Both metaphorically and literally.

No rest, sore boobs, you can't sit down

Visitors round at every hour.

The baby won't sleep unless on you,

And you haven't had a shower

For at least two days, or maybe three...

You're no longer sure at all.

A full-time role without training tips;

It's the hardest job of all.

No, it's nothing like a "year off",

A "break" or "holiday",

But a magical year of enjoying life

In the most exhausting way.

JUST TELL ME I'LL BE OK

Hold me close,

In your maternal way

And please just tell me

I'll be ok.

THEM

They all seemed the same, the ones who blamed

Me for the lack of flexibility, with my modern identity;

Their pack mentality, hunting me down,

When word got around that I did things differently;

Their opinionated eyes, too blind to see,

That this was my baby, not an extension of them.

My treasure, my pearl, my own little gem.

I'd do it my way, with or without their disapproving glares

Preparing the grape vine like bright red flares;

"She's doing it her way again. The wrong way."

SOMETHING HAS MOVED

I'm not sure what it is

But I didn't feel like this

Before I had kids.

Something has moved.

No longer internally screwed

In or through or on.

Shifted up, or around

Except those bits that went down

My internal map is now wrong.

.

MINI ME

Where did you learn that sarcastic tone?

Stomping around like a tiny clone,

Wagging your finger in my face,

Making your own rules like you own the place.

You've a quick-witted response to every action,

Resulting in a flood of comic satisfaction.

Replicating my behaviour, both bad and good;

Evidence I'm succeeding at parenthood.

Procrastinating at every opportunity,

Oh, how you always remind me of me.

Those comments you say, using my inflection

And perfected death stares heading in all directions.

You copy what you hear and what you see me do,

And there are things that *I* do that remind me of you!

My twin, my duplicate, my own imitation,

With perfect idiosyncratic emulation.

A genuine, fool-proof, exact-same copy -

My very own mini-me...

... just a bit more cocky.

DECIDEDLY AVERAGE

More than happy just to be,

In fact, I aspire to be,

Decidedly average.

IT'S OK

He screamed at me

For eating his imaginary

Rainbow ice cream

That he gave me.

He complained at me

That he had no room

When he decided to occupy the majority

Of MY bed.

He cried at me

When I tried to convince him

That the carrots in front of him

Were orange, not red.

He lost it at me

Because I went down the stairs

Before him.

He wanted to be first.

He shouted at me

When I didn't cut up his food

Because it was beans.

He wanted them cut.

He hugged me

And apologised to me

Because he wanted to be good.

But he already was.

And it took

Every ache in my body

To stay calm,

To not shout.

To listen and reassure him

To help him process,

identify, understand

what and how and when

to react.

To the cocktail of emotions.

The flock of butterflies in his body

That escape without prior warning;

Without understanding how to escape.

And it is hard.

Relentless, never ending

Ever changing.

And I guess it's the same for me too.

THEY

I made them a cup of tea,

Whilst the woke our resting baby,

Within hours of just giving birth.

Then they continued to 'advise',

Instruct and chastise,

Thus decreasing our sense of self-worth.

They'd turn up unannounced

And complain about the house,

And the dishes that were sat on the side.

They made us question our choices;

We'd end up raising our voices,

Leaving us feeling unqualified.

Sadly, the 'post-baby assistance'

Seemed to provoke resistance –

They were interfering and meddling again.

"you'd be better doing it our way,

It's what we did in our day."

Well, things have changed since then.

QUESTIONS

The question today:

Do dinosaurs have eyebrows?

I don't have a clue.

FAKING IT

I'm not me, in front of you.

A mish mash of engaged faces,

And excited noises,

And play with this, look at that,

Singing songs,

Rowing boats, winding bobbins,

Stifling yawns

Or holding back tears

For fears that you'll see them

And now that I'm faking it.

With you.

GENDER SCAN

Convinced. Certain.

No doubt in my mind.

Confidently positive.

Frowning at those who 'knew' different.

I secretly knew what you were.

I had planned out our days

Your names, what I'd say

When I shouted for you to come in.

Room decorations, toys,

trips out and skills to learn.

And after being told that I was wrong.

I struggled to feel that you belonged

In my little world I'd created

    -   No, that's understated -

I was disappointed. I'm sorry.

But I was.

I thought that I secretly knew

About you,

But others knew before me.

They knew more about you than I did.

And it hurt.

No longer convinced or certain.

Not confidently positive.

Disappointed.

I'm sorry.

TIRED

In a world where

Instant gratification

Become the sand bags

Against our front door.

Where the pressure

For perfection

Swallows the basic

Necessities for happiness.

Where anything you want

You get yesterday.

A conveyor belt

Of more and more things.

Where time overrules

And interrupts those

Tiny hands clasping

For one more cuddle.

Where expectation

Thwarts ideas

And extinguishes

Dreams.

Where being you

Is taboo.

Unheard of.

Unwanted.

We conform, adhere.

Follow the trend.

Ignore individuality.

Blend.

I'm tired. So tired.

Tired of blending.

Tired of suiting others.

Tired of conforming to

Someone else's ideal.

My little ones will see me

As me. Happy.

Enjoying life

The way I know how.

Where dreams are as

Essential as air.

Where time exists

But only as a guideline

Where those 'just-one-more-cuddles'

Are endless.

Where we can wait

And let the excitement build

Where we are happy

Just

Being

Us.

Together.

Where we are

Good enough.

And are happy being good enough.

Tired, but a different type of tired.

THE BEAUTY OF PETROL STATIONS

It is socially acceptable

To do the unthinkable

And abandon your child in the car.

Whilst you spend two blissful minutes

Perusing varieties of biscuits,

Knowing you're not really that far.

ACCOMPANIED PEEING

If you have two under three,

And you're needing a wee

Then you haven't got a hope in hell.

But if they've got the facility

Then take the opportunity.

Us mums need the toilet as well.

BABY WEIGHT

Can I still refer

To it as baby weight if

My child is seven?

DON'T TOUCH

It's awkward but acceptable,

To ask guests to wash their hands

When they've come to see the newborn

And the majority will understand.

Scientific evidence is out there;

it's about preventing infection.

These tiny humans don't yet have

A fully developed immune system.

So, when you go a-visiting,

Just grab the soap and scrub.

Then everyone will be more relaxed

When you have your squidge with bub.

LIES AND DECEIT

The lies we tell our kids

To make them go to sleep

To put on both their shoes

Or have one more bite to eat.

We compromise, negotiate,

We threaten empty words,

But sometimes kids just refuse

And act like little turds.

OH, WELL DONE!

6,552 hours

Was how long

I was pregnant for.

An you want a medal

For spending 10 minutes

Cleaning the kitchen floor?

IN THE CLUB

We won't share

A secret handshake

Or a knowing nod,

A cryptic password

Or a noise that's odd.

We don't need

To be watched with

Detective glances

From different angles

Because the chance is

You'll be disappointed.

We don't want

To be the topic of

Private conversations.

Discussing details.

Sharing observations.

Because, if and when we know,

And when we're ready,

You'll know.

And if you think

You know already,

Forget it.

Erase it.

A **PARENT'S HEART**

It remains one size

And yet expands with each child.

What is its limit?

SELF-EXPLANATORY

Piles.

Bum grapes.

Bloody Bum Grapes.

Bloody Bastard Bum Grapes.

They hurt.

As if my body isn't going through enough.

Bastards.

MUMMY TUMMY

Exercise, diets and creams

Are futile, or so it would seem.

This crepe paper tummy

(which my son finds quite funny)

Will only be flat in my dreams.

HOME COOKED

Tonight, I felt creative

And made frittata for their tea,

Instead of something from a box.

I thought, "Let's be healthy."

"F ck that." I said, annoyed.

He didn't even try it.

I guess it's just box food forever more.

Ungrateful little sh t.

CHECK IN

A flow of visitors

As soon as we were ready

To meet the newest member,

A stream, slow and steady.

Inboxes full of messages,

Phone calls every day,

Those first two weeks were busy

But the numbers dwindled away.

Flying solo, as he

Returned to work as well.

The once filled rooms

Seemed to swell.

Lost in my own house.

Frantically trying to learn

How to do this alone;

Luckily, the good ones return.

They visit,

They phone,

They offer to help

clean my home.

The others have had their cuddle,

Their photo opportunity.

They've had their fix

Of cooing at the baby.

But then it stops.

The family visits stop.

The friendly phone calls stop.

The 'Just checking-in' texts stop.

The 'I'll help' offers stop.

Those empty promises evaporate.

But, luckily, the good ones return.

THE FOURTH TRIMESTER

Gas and air; I wanted more.

Visitors everywhere

Sending texts, "bring paracetamol"

Hormonal sweating nightmare.

Mastitis. Ready to give up.

A successful school run alone.

A box of formula for back up.

Breastfeeding support on the phone.

The itchy return of piles.

Finally signed off by the midwife.

Those adorable milk drunk smiles.

In awe of this new little life.

Paternity leave abruptly stops

Her weight gain sustained by me.

Comfy leggings and floaty tops.

A few more visits from family.

Oral thrush and nipple cream

A refusal to sleep in her cot.

An organised tag team sleep routine.

Still persevering with the gold top.

Devouring box sets on Netflix.

From maternity pad to liner.

Mastitis is back in the mix.

Morning cuddles. Life couldn't be finer.

Selling stuff on eBay.

Screams whilst in the bath.

Cluster feeding all day long.

This is going way too fast.

My six week check – a brief affair.

My "thoughts on contraception".

Her tongue pokes out purposefully

Another breast infection.

Blocks of sleep, at least an hour.

Coffee dates with friends.

Babywearing saves the day.

My milk-filled boob offends.

Sensory overload at baby class.

Unsuccessful first-time swimming.

A search for nice breastfeeding tops.

Finally, feeling like I'm winning.

Rolling over, front to back,

Her brother pushed her over.

The cutest little giggles.

Wishing time would just go slower.

Ewan the Sheep helps *me* sleep.

The house is a right mess.

A much-needed Mum's Night Out.

Just doing what feels best.

Inquisitive at three months old.

I'm her permanent protector.

Life continues in beautiful chaos,

As we move out of the fourth trimester.

FLOOR FOOD

So, you want to eat it off the floor?

Like you've seen the animals do before.

Throwing each piece from the highchair,

Watching in amusement as a pile slowly grows there.

Refusing to eat it straight from the plate

Yet, plonked on the floor, you think it's great.

A picnic of sorts with extra bits

Nothing that will give you the sh ts

But a few missed crumbs from a previous meal;

Floor food just has a bit more appeal.

Maybe it was too soft or too cold,

Well, now there are bits of old fluff involved.

Either way, you are eating so I'm not really fussed

Just don't tell the health visitor you eat from the dust.

THUNDER BUDDY

Each time you feel

Their breathing relax,

The flash and rumble

Brings the panic right back.

You repeat, "you're safe."

And, "It's ok. I'm here"

Whispering softly

"there's nothing to fear."

Another night interrupted.

Another night with less sleep.

Another night being kicked

By two tiny feet.

Maybe the last, though

When they need their mummy.

You see, you wont always be

Their thunder storm buddy.

Enjoy the moment,

Soak it in, mummy.

Tomorrow can always be

Fuelled by tea or coffee.

For they won't always be small,

They won't always creep

Into your bed when

The nights make them weep.

Soak it in, mummy.

These years go so fast.

Soon nightly disturbances

Will be a thing of the past.

Soak it in, mummy

They grow way too quickly.

One day they won't need you as

Their thunder storm buddy.

MY CELLULITE

Mini fat stores

Of energy

Required to enable me

To continuously

Tirelessly

 Support the spontaneous life

Of a toddler.

Thank you, cellulite.

You're a bit like nose hairs...

Unsightly but important.

THE ASSUMPTION OF ANOTHER

At first there was no assumption of one,

No expectation, no anticipation.

Now that one is here, they expect two

Like buses, "When's the next one due?"

We need time to adjust and reorganise

But they badger on about our family size.

Watching and waiting for tiny clues,

Always expecting exciting news.

"She had a lemonade rather than wine.

What does it mean? Is it a sign?"

Why can't we be happy with just one?

Maybe as three, we're complete, we're done.

They can't see the past or what it took

To be able to hold this one in the crook

Of our arms.

And still they assume

They know the future of my womb.

Don't assume there'll be another

Just because she's now a mother.

We're happy,

Just us three.

DON'T DO IT!

Hand on the handle

Jeans by your knees

Dilemmas faced by every mum

When you're trying to pee

In public toilets.

We've all been there.

LADY GARDEN

I can no longer see it

But I know it's everywhere,

And who knows *who* will see it

When they take a look down there.

It's getting closer to the date,

And I'm more and more aware;

You see, I'm having trouble deciding

How to style my pubic hair.

A landing strip, a postage stamp

Or going completely bare;

I'm scared they'll confuse my bush

For the crowning baby's hair.

There's a few things I fret about

When I'm inhaling gas and air.

Including an accidental poo

and resembling a bear.

Is it possible to birth a child

Whilst wearing underwear?

Why am I panicking?

They've all seen their fair share.

And when I'm in the final moments

Will I seriously even care?

I'll be busy pushing a baby out

And trying not to swear.

Midwives do this every day;

My muff will not impair

Their concentration and attention,

On what's happening down there.

And once that baby is in my arms,

With my legs still in the air,

The last thing on my mind will be

The state of my pubic hair.

DISGUSTING

You know what *IS* disgusting...

Food caught in a man's beard from three days ago.

Bad breath, especially first in the morning.

Day light robbery on those who are vulnerable.

Farting with no apology, no warning.

Overflowing bins in a public park.

A fridge full of rotting food, when half the world is hungry.

Dog poo that's been left on the street for others to step in.

Empty drug canisters littered from a sporadic outdoor party.

A t-shirt that no longer covers that expanse of belly flesh.

Racism in a world that should always embrace colour.

Politicians who prioritise wealth over health.

Hatred to those who, in austerity, have shown valour.

Fly tipping in places of natural beauty.

Adults who believe that peeing in public is acceptable.

Hate mail and trolling to make others feel down.

Looters who believe that stealing is commendable.

But, do you know what's not disgusting..?

Breastfeeding.

Breastfeeding is not disgusting.

So, don't you dare make anyone feel that way

With the disgustingly negative comments you say.

It's natural; in public, at home, wherever.

It brings mum and baby closer together.

So, keep your horrible thoughts to yourself.

Better yet, go and eat your lunch somewhere else.

I can recommend the toilet, or maybe a dark room?

Or a sheet on your head just in case you might swoon

From the sight of a baby having lunch from a breast;

Just keep those disgusting thoughts close to your chest.

And if my message has not really quite sunk in,

That breastfeeding is definitely not disgusting,

Then take this one thought, from me to you...

_ _ _ _   _ _ _

(fill in the blanks – it's simple to do.)

WHO WE ONCE WERE

She's not gone, not forgotten.

Just temporarily hidden.

Like the smarties inside a cake,

Not put there by mistake,

covered in layers of life.

And iced

With experience.

Like a pas the parcel

Knowing she can unravel

When the music stops,

When the music changes.

A woman with a new agenda,

Not her ideal all night bender

But a dance for two.

For them both it's new.

She once partied 'til dawn,

And she could have sworn

She had a list of things to do

Before...

But...

She'd not lost, she's there

And when her favourite song comes on

She'll still dance anywhere

Without a care.

For she IS still there

That glimmer, that spark.

Now stronger, more defined

No longer undermined

But true to herself.

A new sense of wealth.

Not financial – it would be nice –

But an experience of life.

Creating life.

The best all nightery.

Saturated with laughter.

Becoming a mother.

In it, and then the party after

Where she'll be released again.

And she will dance.

And given a chance

She'll dance like there's no tomorrow.

New moves, different groves

Inspired by older hips

Slightly saggier bits.

She'd not gone, not even close.

The 'you' you once were

Will always be there

If you want it.

FANNY PHYSIO

Assessing my dysfunctional parts,

A referral is where this all starts.

Retraining my pelvic floor

(Nothing I'd heard of before)

And massaging scars that I swore

Would prevent me from ever having sex,

But here, what's next?

Internal manual therapy

To stop the accidental wee!

What can this magic be?

Physio... for my fanny.

Like what you've read?

Follow me:

@postpartumpoet (Instagram)

@postpartumpoetry (Facebook)

www.postpartumpoetry.co.uk

Printed in Great Britain
by Amazon